I Feel Worried

Written by Brian Moses
Illustrated by Mike Gordon

sundance
A Haights Cross Communications Company

Kid-to-Kid Books

Red Set	Green Set	Blue Set	Yellow Set
I Feel Angry	I Feel Bored	I Feel Bullied	Excuse Me!
I Feel Happy	I Feel Jealous	I Feel Frightened	I Don't Care!
I Feel Lonely	I Feel Shy	I Feel Sad	I'll Do It!
It's Not Fair	I Feel Worried	Why Wash?	It Wasn't Me!

All rights reserved.
This edition published
in North America by
Sundance Publishing
P.O. Box 740
One Beeman Road
Northborough, MA 01532

First published in 1997 by
Wayland Publishers Limited

Copyright © 1997 Wayland Publishers Limited

ISBN 0-7608-3917-4

sundance
A Haights Cross Communications Company

Printed in China

In the corner today,
we're talking about

feeling worried.

This way to Kids Corner

3

When I feel worried,
I feel like

a dog that
can't find his bone,

4

a balloon that's
losing its air,

a bird that knows
there's a cat
out there somewhere.

5

When I feel worried,

there's a rain cloud over my head,

there are butterflies in my tummy,

my face wears
a frown,

I can't concentrate
on my work
at school.

When my friends don't want
to play with me,
and I don't know why,
I feel worried.

But soon I find
someone else to play with.

When I have to read my poem out loud,
and everyone is looking at me,
I feel worried.

But once I start reading,
I begin to like it.

When the doctor says
I have to have my tonsils out,
I feel worried.

But Mom will be there
to hold my hand.

When I have to take
a swimming test,
I feel worried.

But when everyone cheers for me,
I forget how worried I was.

When my rabbit is sick
and won't eat his food,
I feel worried.

But the vet says,
"Don't worry.
He'll be all right
in a day or two."

Sometimes grown-ups say,

"Stop worrying. Snap out of it."

"You're a big girl now. Be brave. There's nothing to worry about."

But grown-ups feel worried, too.

"Is there enough
money to pay
all the bills?"

Sometimes I make other people worry —

like when I walk
along a high wall,

or when I don't look both ways
before I cross the street.

When I feel worried,
it helps if I think
about something fun,

like a trip to the movies,

or a game with Dad,

or playing
on the computer.

It helps if I can talk
to someone
about my worries.

Sometimes
I even talk to Ben
from next door.

Sometimes
a worry turns out
not to be a worry at all.
And sometimes,
if you wait a while,
a worry just goes away.

Do you ever
feel worried?
What makes you
feel better?

Things to Do in the Kids Corner

Here's a good way to "wipe away your worries." On a chalkboard, write a sentence about something that makes you feel worried. Now erase it! You can do this whenever you feel worried!

Work with a friend. Find these words in the book: *when, feel, cloud, friends, hand, snap, about, wall,* and *trip*. Write the words. Circle a smaller word in each of the words you wrote.

Write the letters *w, o, r, r, i, e,* and *d* down the side of a piece of lined paper. On each line, write three words that begin with that letter. Compare your words with a friend's.

Read *I Feel Worried* to a friend. Ask your friend to stand up each time you read a word that rhymes with *may*. How many times did your friend stand? Pick another book and switch jobs. How many times did you stand up?

Draw a picture about a time when you felt worried. Share your picture with a friend. Tell your friend what you did to feel better.

Other Books to Read

Gila Monsters Meet You at the Airport, by Marjorie Weinman Sharmat (Simon and Schuster, 1990). Moving to a new house, in a new town, in a new state can be a little scary. Not knowing what to expect at your new home can really make you feel worried. When a small boy moves west to the desert from his home in New York City, his imagination runs wild. *30 pages*

Last Look, by Clyde R. Bulla (Penguin Books, 1995). Monica becomes worried when the new girl in her class disappears. The missing girl has left a mysterious note just for Monica. What does it all mean? *80 pages*

Lily, by Abigail Thomas (Henry Holt, 1997). Lily watches as Eliza packs everything up in boxes. Lily and Eliza are moving from an apartment in Boston to a house in Vermont. And the move is making Lily feel pretty worried. *32 pages*

Never Spit on Your Shoes, by Denys Cazet (Orchard Books, 1993). All the joy and fun and fears and worries of starting first grade come to life as Arnie tells his mother about the first day of school. *32 pages*

Sarah, Plain and Tall, by Patricia MacLachlan (HarperCollins, 1985). When Caleb and Anna's father needed a new wife, he put an ad in the newspaper. Now Sarah is coming from Maine to join their family. Will she like them? Will they like her? Caleb, Anna, their Papa, and Sarah all worry about how their new family arrangement will work out. *58 pages*